The Bald Eagle's View

of American H

The Bald Eagle's View of American History

C. H. Colman

Illustrated by Joanne Friar

Charlesbridge

To my parents, John and Rebecca Colman—C. H. C.

To my sons Chris and Jim, for their love of nature

and appreciation of history—J. F.

Stamps used courtesy of the United States Postal Service.
All rights reserved. See p. 47 for full copyright information.

Text copyright © 2006 by C. H. Colman
Illustrations copyright © 2006 by Joanne Friar
All rights reserved, including the right of reproduction in whole or in part in any form.
Charlesbridge and colophon are registered trademarks of Charlesbridge Publishing, Inc.

Published by Charlesbridge
85 Main Street
Watertown, MA 02472
(617) 926-0329
www.charlesbridge.com

Library of Congress Cataloging-in-Publication Data
Colman, C. H.
　　The bald eagle's view of American history / C.H. Colman; illustrated by Joanne Friar.
　　　　p. cm.
　　Summary: "Tells the history of the United States from a bald eagle's point of view and
features postage stamps that chronicle historic events. Includes factual back matter about bald
eagles and postage stamps as well as a bibliography"—Provided by publisher.
　　ISBN-13: 978-1-58089-300-8; ISBN-10: 1-58089-300-7 (reinforced for library use)
　　ISBN-13: 978-1-58089-301-5; ISBN-10: 1-58089-301-5 (softcover)
1. United States—On postage stamps—Juvenile literature. 2. United States—History—Pictorial
works—Juvenile literature. 3. Bald eagle—United States—Pictorial works—Juvenile literature.
4. History on postage stamps—Juvenile literature. 5. Birds on postage stamps—Juvenile
literature.　　I. Friar, Joanne H., ill.　II. Title.
　HE6183.U54C65 2006
　973—dc22　　　　　　　　　　　2005019626

Printed in China
(hc) 10 9 8 7 6 5 4 3 2 1
(sc) 10 9 8 7 6 5 4 3 2 1

Illustrations done in watercolor and colored pencils on Fabriano paper
Display type set in P22 Mayflower and text type set in Adobe Caslon
Color separated, printed, and bound by Everbest Printing Company, Ltd.,
　　through Four Colour Imports Ltd., Louisville, Kentucky
Production supervision by Brian G. Walker
Designed by Susan Mallory Sherman

Contents

Foreword

Stamps have mesmerized me since I started my first collection at age five. I remember looking at my favorite issues of commemorative stamps and imagining the events detailed in those tiny pictures. For me, stamps are more than the means to post a letter. They are works of art that often celebrate national milestones, symbols, or prominent people.

I wanted to use stamps to help illustrate my history of America. I searched through a stamp catalog to find the theme with which to knit events. Many stamps showed the bald eagle, America's national emblem. Here was a fitting viewpoint: eagle ecology intersects much of our experience, starting with the arrival of humans on this continent. The big birds have inspired us with their power and grace, freedom and skill. Research produced relevant historical examples of such inspiration.

I hope this book will introduce you to the sweep of American history while showing how humans make a difference to a species' existence, in both harmful and helpful ways. In addition maybe some of you will come to love stamps. Perhaps you will even start a collection and embark on one of life's best journeys.

Eagles in America

For thousands of years bald eagles have soared above America. The white-headed bird watched branches break and rocks roll when Ice Age glaciers smashed forests and scooped out lakes.

Eagles flew overhead when the first people arrived.

The First Americans

A bald eagle sailed above the Bering land bridge, turning its head to look into the eyes of a human. A glint from the river lured the bird. It swooped, sank its talons into a salmon, and plucked it from the water. The human ran to the bank, smelling the wet grass and yelling. He speared enough salmon to feed himself and his companions.

Those humans stayed in their new land and became the first Native Americans.

Hunters and Warriors

For several thousand years bald eagles soared above the native people. Eagles stroked the air as they searched for the same food the humans hunted.

One bald eagle dove toward a wolf's exposed flesh. A hunter hid in his pit below the dead animal's outstretched skin, breathing the nutty scents of earth and dry grass. The eagle hovered, stretching out one talon, then another, before landing on its meal. The bird screamed as the hunter jerked it underground. A warrior bartered for the feathers that he wore to help him fight with the strength of an eagle.

European Settlers Arrive

The native people lost most of their lands when Europeans settled in America. First the Vikings came, but they only stayed a short time. Then the Spanish, Dutch, British, and French arrived. Dutch families started the settlement that later became America's biggest city when they came to Manhattan in 1624. They traded with the natives for beaver fur. Bald eagles ate fish on Hudson River ice floes as breezes turned the sails on the town windmill. The Dutch lost their town of New Amsterdam in a war with the British, who renamed the property New York.

The British also named the eagle "bald,"

a word that then had several meanings, including "white patch." At that time there were as many bald eagles living in America as people living in today's city of Boston (about 589,000).

Over the next hundred years, ships carried thousands of settlers, mainly British, to America's East Coast. The colonists built towns and planted crops, pushing bald eagles from many of their hunting and breeding areas.

American Independence

People had not yet settled a stretch of the Delaware River where, one cool summer morning in 1776, a bald eagle dove and hooked a large fish. The fish dragged the bird under. The eagle beat its wings like paddle wheels on a riverboat, rising to the surface in time to breathe. The bird thrashed until it dragged its catch ashore.

That afternoon, in nearby Philadelphia, representatives from the thirteen British colonies signed Thomas Jefferson's Declaration of Independence from Britain. Through the long years of the Revolutionary War that followed, Americans would often

feel as if they, too, were drowning. However, like the bald eagle, the former colonies kept fighting.

15

The National Emblem

In 1782, a year before George Washington led America to victory in the Revolutionary War, Congress chose the country's national emblem, ending a long debate.

Benjamin Franklin thought he would like the turkey as the national emblem. He wrote to his daughter that, though a little silly, a turkey would not hesitate to defend its farmyard from a British soldier's attack.

Thomas Jefferson favored the bald eagle and admired its courage. Eagle parents defend their nest against predators, though not always against humans. What is more, although eagles prefer fishing, they battle other birds for food.

Benjamin Franklin thought the bald eagle was a thief.

Thomas Jefferson admired the bald eagle when it soared to great heights.

Benjamin Franklin's letter did not mention the turkey's flying skills. A wild turkey takes off like a helicopter and flies, for a little way, as fast as a car moves along a highway. A bald eagle stays aloft for hours looking for food before plunging at twice the turkey's flying speed.

Congress chose the bald eagle as the national emblem. Its freedom to soar brought to mind the freedom from Britain that most Americans wanted. The eagle's fighting skills suggested America's similar struggle for independence.

The Louisiana Purchase

The United States was now a young nation, stretching along the East Coast of America. France owned the center of the continent, which it called Louisiana. This was a huge area, far larger than today's state of the same name.

Bald eagles had the freedom to fly anywhere in Louisiana, raising their chicks beside every large river and lake, and living in balance with the native people. Such freedom was about to change.

In 1803 the United States, under President Thomas Jefferson, bought Louisiana from the French ruler, Napoleon. Napoleon could not defend his property in the New World and needed money to spend on his war against Britain. The money didn't help Napoleon, who lost the war, but the purchase allowed the United States to stretch toward the Pacific.

The Lewis and Clark Expedition

President Jefferson sent Meriwether Lewis and William Clark to find a route across the Louisiana Purchase to the Pacific Ocean.

Bald eagles watched the expedition pole its boats up the Missouri River. One bald eagle, living on an island, peered through the mist as the explorers reached Black Eagle Falls in what is now Montana. As Lewis and Clark headed home after reaching the Pacific Ocean, they searched for food. A bald eagle dropped a salmon that was too heavy for the bird to carry to its nest. The salmon fed the members of the expedition.

Westward Movement

Waves of settlers flowed along Lewis and Clark's path or found other routes west. Bald eagles flew overhead as men chopped trees. Nests crashed; the smell of sawdust lingered. Fallen wood became houses and barns and fences. Farms replaced forests. New states formed and joined the Union.

The Civil War

Yet Northern states disagreed with Southern states on many things, especially slavery. These problems led to the American Civil War in the 1860s.

During the Civil War, a Wisconsin regiment adopted a bald eagle. The soldiers called the bird Old Abe, after their president, Abraham Lincoln. Members of the regiment loved Old Abe, even though the eagle tore uniforms drying on the clothesline. Old Abe screamed warnings when the enemy attacked. The big bird dodged bullets, or flew just above them, in 36 battles. After the Northern states won the war, Old Abe lived for 16 more years.

Other bald eagles were not as lucky.
Settlers continued to spread across the country, changing the land. Engineers built a dam
across Black Eagle Falls. By 1900 the number
of bald eagles living in America equaled half
the population in today's city of Boston.

Airplanes Share the Skies

Bald eagles still flew above the shores of North Carolina when Wilbur and Orville Wright brought their glider there in 1900. A salty breeze sang from the sea. The brothers discussed how eagles and other birds could soar and stay over one part of the beach without flapping their wings.

The Wrights believed that the eagles and other birds achieved a perfect balance among wings that lift, breezes that push, and gravity that pulls. The brothers thought that if they built a glider that could soar and remain stationary as the eagles did, they could attach an engine to it and fly.

One day Wilbur climbed onto his glider, soared into the air, and remained stationary for 43 seconds.

The Wrights built an engine, bolted it to another glider, and attached propellers.

In 1903 Orville steered his mechanical bird above the shore, engine smoke racing over icy puddles.

The Wrights had taught humans how to fly with the eagles.

The Screaming Eagles

29
USA

Airborne units spearhead attacks, 1944

Americans discovered so much about flying that, by 1917, U.S. planes were fighting in the First World War.

After the war the army introduced parachutes so soldiers could float through the air and surprise an enemy. The 101st Infantry Division, which wore patches showing Old Abe, the Civil War eagle, became the 101st Airborne Division. The new paratroopers kept the patch and called themselves the Screaming Eagles because they wanted to fight like Old Abe. The state of Wisconsin gave the 101st a live bald eagle. The paratroopers named their mascot Young Abe.

27

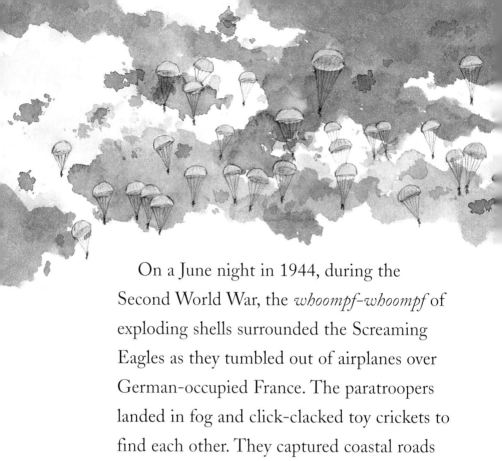

On a June night in 1944, during the Second World War, the *whoompf-whoompf* of exploding shells surrounded the Screaming Eagles as they tumbled out of airplanes over German-occupied France. The paratroopers landed in fog and click-clacked toy crickets to find each other. They captured coastal roads from the Germans. In the morning American infantrymen leaped out of boats and stormed ashore. They raced up the roads, waving to the Screaming Eagles, and began freeing France from its enemy.

Back in America, bald eagles were to face a different type of enemy.

Endangered Eagles

AMERICAN BALD EAGLE

After the Second World War, farmers started using a new chemical, DDT, to kill crop insects. Rain washed DDT into rivers and lakes, where plants absorbed it. Fish ate the plants, swallowing DDT, and bald eagles ate the fish. DDT thinned the shells of eagle eggs, which broke before they hatched. By the 1960s eagles had left the Wright brothers' beach and no longer nested along the Delaware River. There were now fewer bald eagles living in the lower forty-eight states than people living on one Boston street: under 900 birds remained.

At the same time that eagles were dying,

scientists were perfecting a new form of flying: the rocket.

President John F. Kennedy thought about the possibilities of rockets, and he also thought about the distress of the bald eagle. He challenged Americans to do two things.

One of them was to fly to the moon.

The other was to save the national emblem.

The Eagle on the Moon

People around the world, some of whom had been alive when the Wrights first flew, switched on their TV sets in 1969 when Americans reached the moon.

"The Eagle has wings," said Neil Armstrong. He turned his small lander, named the Eagle in honor of America's symbol, away from the mother ship and flew toward a gray surface. The sun glared like lights at a football game as the Eagle's engines flashed, and the dust flew.

Armstrong eased the lander past a boulder and spoke again. "The Eagle has landed."

Neil Armstrong and Edwin "Buzz" Aldrin

opened the hatch and placed the first human footprints on the moon. Their blue boots brought back dust that smelled like gunpowder from fireworks.

Saving Our National Emblem

After the moon landing, Americans found ways to save the national emblem. The government banned DDT in 1972, having already declared the bald eagle an endangered species in 1967. Naturalists brought the big bird back to some of the places it had left.

By 2003 there were as many bald eagles living in the continental United States as people living on a dozen streets in Boston, or about 13,000 birds.

Once again, an eagle hovers above the Wright brothers' beach.

Another eagle dives into the Delaware.

The bird that looked into the eyes of the
first American is free to watch over America.

35

Time Line

40,000 BCE

Bald eagle tar pit fossils

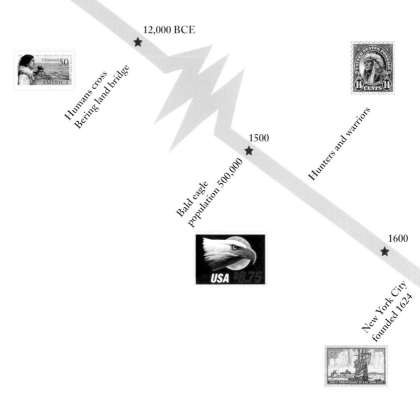

12,000 BCE

Humans cross Bering land bridge

Hunters and warriors

1500

Bald eagle population 500,000

1600

New York City founded 1624

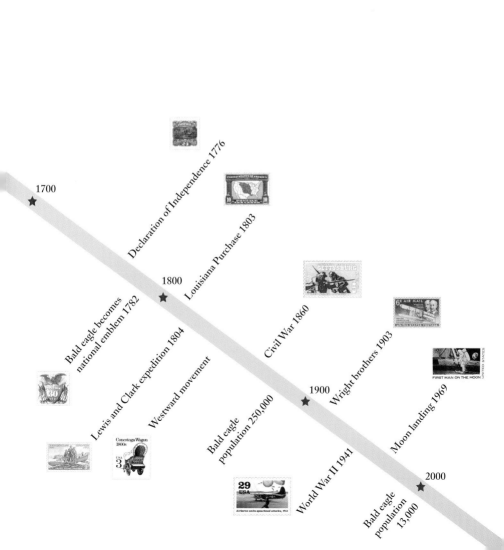

1700

Declaration of Independence 1776

Louisiana Purchase 1803

1800

Bald eagle becomes
national emblem 1782

Lewis and Clark expedition 1804

Westward movement

Civil War 1860

Wright brothers 1903

Bald eagle
population 250,000

1900

Moon landing 1969

World War II 1941

2000

Bald eagle
population
13,000

Author's Notes

The Stamps

The United States Postal Service issued all
the stamps shown in this book. The oldest
stamps are Declaration of Independence and
Shield, Eagle, Flags, both from 1869. Today
each of these stamps is worth hundreds of
dollars. However, you can buy some of this
book's stamps for about a dollar.

Stamps allow people to appreciate a country's history and culture. Collecting began in
England in 1840 when that country issued
the world's first stamp. One in ten people
save stamps, making it by far the biggest collecting hobby. If you would like to find out

more, visit the United States Postal Service website at www.usps.com and look for the Collector's Corner in the Postal Store. If you go to Washington, D.C., stop by the National Postal Museum where you can see most U.S. stamps and tour exhibits that explain the history of mail.

The Story

Our national emblem is all around. Whether soaring above the countryside or looking forward from its painting on the postal van, the big bird reminds us of its power and grace. The sources listed below refer interested readers to more detailed works about the bald eagle and the events described in this book.

Bald eagles have lived in North America for thousands of years. California tar pits yield bald eagle fossils from the late Pleistocene epoch, up to 40,000 years BCE. The Page Museum's informative website at www.tarpits.org describes one of these pits, the La Brea.

Bald eagles are primarily fish and carrion eaters and probably searched for the same food as the earliest people. Freeman House, in his book *Totem Salmon* (Beacon Press, 1999, p. 9), theorizes that salmon in Alaska's glacial rivers attracted early man to North America. Professor Timothy Heaton has excavated a partial bald eagle skeleton from Dall Island, Alaska, dating it as 8,740 years old, but believes that bald eagles have been in coastal Alaska since long before the last glacial maximum, predating the arrival of humans. You can read about the main fossils that Professor Heaton has excavated at www.usd.edu/~theaton.

George Grinnell, in *The Cheyenne Indians* (Yale University Press, 1923, vol. 1, p. 299), provides a detailed account of how Native Americans hunted bald eagles.

When Europeans arrived in North America, there were about half a million bald eagles, as stated by *National Geographic* in its wonderfully visual July 2002 article "Majesty in Motion." Greg Breining echoes this estimate in his book *Return of the Eagle* (Falcon Press, 1994, p. 40). In comparing the bald eagle population to the human population of Boston, I used the United States Census 2000 estimate of 589,000.

Bald eagles once nested along every large river and concentration of lakes from Labrador in Canada to Florida, and from Baja California in Mexico to Alaska. The birds lived along the Hudson River when the Dutch arrived. Windmill Tower, a famous landmark of the early Manhattan settlement, is positioned on the left side of the New York City stamp. Dorothy Hinshaw Patent, in her excellent children's book *The Bald Eagle Returns* (Clarion, 2000, p. 33), states that as late as 1850, bald eagles would fish in the Hudson and carry their prey to Central Park. Today the birds once again fish from Hudson River ice floes.

Daniel Brauning, head of Pennsylvania's Bald Eagle Recovery Program, confirmed the presence of bald eagles around Philadelphia at the time of the Declaration of Independence, as well as the bird's recent return to that area. In addition, Dan was kind enough to advise me on the eagle habits described in this book.

Benjamin Franklin's preference for the turkey over the bald eagle as national emblem is well-known. Franklin actually stated his views to his daughter on January 26, 1784, per *The Writings of Benjamin Franklin* (Macmillan, 1906, vol. IX), nineteen months after Congress chose the eagle.

My description of bald eagle interactions with the Lewis and Clark expedition comes from accounts based on Meriwether Lewis's journal, as published in *History of the Expedition under the Command of Captains Lewis and Clark,* edited by Paul Allen (Bradford and Inskeep, 1814). Lewis and Clark reached Black Eagle Falls on June 14,

1805 (vol. 1, p. 264). The salmon drop took place on May 18, 1806 (vol. 2, p. 296). You can view pictures of Black Eagle Falls, before and after the building of a dam, at www.lewis-clark.org.

J. M. Williams relates the account of Old Abe, the Civil War eagle, in *The Eagle Regiment,* a book printed by the Belleville, WI, newspaper, *Recorder,* in 1890. I used the Gettysburg stamp as representative of the Civil War, although Old Abe was not present at that battle.

From first European contact, settlers saw the bald eagle as competition for food and a stealer of chickens. People destroyed bald eagle habitats and shot the birds. The bald eagle population declined to 250,000 by 1900, according to Mark Stalmaster in *Bald Eagle* (Universe Books, 1987, p. 29).

There are many references to bald eagles at Kitty Hawk. James Tobin, in *To Conquer the Air* (Free Press, 2003, pp. 146–147) tells how the Wright brothers' observations of carrion eaters and birds of prey led to a belief that artificial wings could be as good as a bird's. Wilbur Wright, in *Miracle at Kitty Hawk: The Letters of Wilbur and Orville Wright* (Farrar, Straus and Young, 1951, p. 36), compared the soaring ability of buzzards to that of eagles. Marcia Lyons, of the National Park Service, confirmed the renewed presence of bald eagles over Kitty Hawk.

J. B. Davies provides an excellent description of the 101st Airborne Division at Normandy in *Great Campaigns of World War II* (Exeter, 1980).

Following World War II, farmers introduced the pesticide DDT, dropping a billion pounds of the toxic chemical before the U.S. government banned its use in 1972. DDT was largely responsible for the near extinction of bald eagles in the Lower 48; the Alaska/Canada eagle population stayed around 50,000. By 1963 the U.S. Fish and

Wildlife Service estimated there were only 417 nesting pairs of bald eagles in the Lower 48. More information is available at www.fws.gov.

President Kennedy wrote to the Audubon Society (*Audubon* magazine, September– October 1961) on July 17, 1961, supporting that organization's initiative to protect the bald eagle: ". . . [A]s latter day citizens we shall have failed a trust if we permit the Eagle to disappear."

Buzz Aldrin provided most of the moon-landing detail in his book *Men from Earth* (Bantam, 1989, p. 234 and following).

Various organizations and states started bald eagle recovery programs in the 1970s and 1980s. Those programs often succeeded. The eagle population grew to 4,500 nesting pairs in 1994. In 1995 the U.S. Fish and Wildlife Service upgraded the status of the bald eagle to threatened, making it one of a handful of species to fight back from the endangered list. A 1999 proposal that is still pending will remove the bald eagle from the list of threatened wildlife in the Lower 48 as well. As of 2003, there were approximately 6,500 nesting pairs of bald eagles in the Lower 48 of the United States.

Today and Tomorrow

If you would like to watch a bald eagle, the Washington Department of Fish and Wildlife has eagle cams at www.wdfw.wa .gov/wildwatch. If you would like to travel to see bald eagles, the website www .recreation.gov provides a state-by-state listing of wildlife refuges.

Today environmentalists continue to help the bald eagle, while developing plans to save all endangered species. The U.S. Fish and Wildlife Service provides details of its programs, including a Kids' Corner, at www.endangered.fws.gov. The Nature

Conservancy, a private organization at www.nature.org, also helps the bald eagle.

Acknowledgments

Many people helped me create this book. In addition to those recognized in my author's notes, I wish to thank the following: specialist James O'Donnell of the National Postal Museum, Smithsonian Institution; from The Nature Conservancy, John Wiens, chief scientist, and Jan V. Portman; the helpful staff in the Rare Book Room of the Public Library of Cincinnati and Hamilton County.

Personal thanks are owed to my wife, Pam, my son David, and my daughter, Laura.

Index